CRYSTALS

Richard Spilsb

Published in paperback in Great Britain in 2019 by Wayland

Copyright © Hodder and Stoughton, 2016

Editors: Sarah Eason and Tim Cooke
Cover design: Lisa Peacock

Produced for Wayland by Calcium
All rights reserved.
ISBN: 978 1 5263 0204 5
10 9 8 7 6 5 4 3 2 1

Wayland
An imprint of
Hachette Children's Group
Part of Hodder & Stoughton
Carmelite House
50 Victoria Embankment
London EC4Y 0DZ

An Hachette UK Company
www.hachette.co.uk

www.hachettechildrens.co.uk

Picture acknowledgements:

Key: b=bottom, t=top, r=right, l=left, m=middle, bgd=background

Picture credits: Cover: Shutterstock: LVV; Inside: Dreamstime: Uldis Bindris 4b, Cornelius20 20r, Dinozzaver 8r, Zsolt Bota Finna 21, Ekaterina Fribus 5b, Gavinp101 18–19, Hotshotsworldwide 17t, Gnel Karapetyan 7b, Ingemar Magnusson 14l, 22b, Carlos Soler Martinez 13t, Milahelp SRO 13b, Tatiana Morozova 14r, 15l, Peter Sobolev 25r, Jennifer Thompson 9c, Vicente Barcelo Varona 19t, Edward Westmacott 16, Simon Zenger 12; Shutterstock: Aarrows 20c, Baloncici 24–25, Fotana 27t, Jorg Hackemann 27b, Imfoto 23, 24t, Gil. K 26r, Lukiyanova Natalia/Frenta 6t, David Reilly 10–11, MarcelClemens 15r, J. Palys 22t, Albert Russ 1, 4t, Siim Sepp 6b, T.W. van Urk 9b, Kozoriz Yuriy 11.

CONTENTS

CRYSTALS

If you use a magnifying glass to study a bowl of salt, you may notice that many of the pieces are shaped like cubes, with flat sides. What you are seeing are crystals!

ROCK SOLID

Big or small, common or rare, all crystals are solid structures. Every crystal has sharp, clear edges and corners. Many crystals have a particular number of flat faces, or sides. Snowflakes are crystals that form when droplets of water in clouds freeze. Every snowflake is different, but each has six arms, or points.

ice crystals

COMMON CRYSTALS

Ice crystals are unusual because most of Earth's crystals are made from **minerals**. These are natural substances that make up the rocks of our planet. The mineral crystals in many rocks are so tiny we cannot see them. However, in rocks like granite, minerals are larger. Mineral crystals can only grow large enough to see without a magnifying glass if they have space and time. That is why we often find crystals in caves. These crystals have grown undisturbed for a long time.

amethyst crystal

gypsum crystal

ROCK STAR STORIES

In 2008, miners in Mexico were hunting for a useful mineral called gypsum when they found an enormous cave deep underground. Inside they found the largest crystals ever discovered. Some of the crystals were 10 metres long and looked like giant white tree trunks! Scientists think the mega-crystals may be half a million years old.

FROM THE DEEP

Deep, deep underground it is far hotter than at Earth's surface, even on a scorching summer's day. It is hot enough for rocks to melt into a mix of minerals called **magma**. Most rock crystals are made from magma.

RISING AND SETTING

Have you watched the blobs of coloured wax in a lava lamp? The wax rises as it heats up. That is what happens to hot magma deep underground. Magma rises through existing spaces in underground rock. It also melts new channels through rock. As it rises, magma travels further from Earth's hot centre. Once magma reaches the surface, it is called lava. When it cools down, the minerals in lava **crystallise** to form solid pieces.

lava

GROWING TOGETHER

The building blocks of all crystals, minerals and anything else on Earth are called **atoms**. Groups of atoms are called **molecules**. In crystals, atoms or molecules are packed together in a very organised way, a little like the way eggs are packed into an egg carton. One carton can sit on another because each egg takes up a particular amount of space. As atoms and molecules from magma are packed together in this organised way, they stack up on top of each other. The molecules and atoms then link together. Over time, these linked rows of molecules and atoms form crystals in rock.

Earth becomes hotter and hotter towards its central core.

Clues to the Past

Diamonds are incredibly tough crystals. They are made of **carbon** atoms that are tightly linked together. Diamonds can only form naturally around 160 kilometres where it is very, very hot. The atoms are forced together by the great **pressure** of the magma around them and the rock above them. Diamonds at the surface of Earth all formed deep underground at least one billion years ago. Magma carried them to the surface during **volcanic eruptions.**

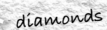

diamonds

SOLUTIONS

Have you ever watched a rock pool dry up in the sun and wind? Did you notice a dusting of white on the rock, just above the water level? If so, then you witnessed another way in which crystals form: when they grow from **solutions**.

This salt has crystallised from seawater by evaporation.

IN A SOLUTION

Nearly all solutions are liquids in which one substance has **dissolved** (mixed with) another substance. Seawater is a solution of salt that has dissolved in water. Many minerals dissolve best in hot water. Water trickles deep underground and heats up as it gets nearer hot magma. It is then better able to dissolve minerals.

CRYSTALS BY MAGIC

Energy in moving air and in the sun's heat also affect water molecules in rock pools. It changes water from a liquid into a gas called **water vapour**. This process is called **evaporation**. When the water changes into a gas, it rises into the air.

Only the salt molecules that were present in the liquid are left behind. The molecules bunch into larger crystals as the water disappears. The crystals are the white substance you notice on the side of empty rock pools.

Some rocks have long **veins** (lines) of crystals such as quartz inside them. These are clues that quartz mineral solutions were once trapped in cracks in the rock. Over time, the water evaporated and the quartz molecules that were left behind formed crystals that filled the remaining space.

quartz vein

ROCK STAR STORIES

making sea salt

In 1866, a miner drilling for oil in rocks near Lake Ontario, Canada, found salt instead! Geologists now know that this Goderich salt deposit covers more than 7.7 square kilometres, making it the largest salt deposit in the world. It formed when water in an ancient sea evaporated. Over many millions of years, the salt molecules left behind became trapped under many layers of rock.

CAVE CRYSTALS

People who explore underground caves find some of the most amazing crystals on Earth. Caves are natural, dark spaces where crystals can grow undisturbed, and with plenty of space, for many thousands of years.

ROCK-EATING RAIN

Did you know that many caves form because of rainwater? Rainwater dissolves a gas called carbon dioxide. This gas is found in air. When rainwater and carbon dioxide mix, it makes a solution that is as **acidic** as lemon juice. If it touches a soft rock called limestone, the solution dissolves a mineral in the rock called calcite. Little by little, the water eats into cracks in the rock, dissolving more and more of it, until a cave forms. Then, as more calcite-rich water drips into the cave, amazing crystals form, too.

stalactites

CRYSTAL TOWERS

Calcite droplets on the cave roof evaporate, leaving behind tiny calcite crystals. Over time, more calcite builds up around the first crystal. This creates long structures called stalactites, which hang down from the cave ceiling. More and more calcite-rich water drips over the stalactite and down onto the cave floor. Inch by inch, calcite towers called stalagmites grow upwards, towards the stalactites.

Clues to the Past

In Mexico, gypsum crystals developed into the largest crystals ever found on Earth. These crystals needed certain conditions to grow. For around half a million years, the limestone caves were filled with a very strong gypsum solution. Nearby magma kept the solution warm, at a constant temperature of 50° centigrade. In these perfect crystal-growing conditions, more and more gypsum crystallised from the solution, and grew into huge crystals.

gypsum crystals

CRYSTAL SHAPE

How can we tell crystals apart? After all, there are around 3,000 types of minerals on our planet, and in the right conditions, each can form crystals. One way to spot the difference is by their shape.

SHAPES AND SYMMETRY

All crystals are **symmetrical**. This means that the faces on one side of the crystal are the same shape as those on the opposite side. This is because crystals grow in a regular way. However, different types of crystals have different shapes. They also have different ways of being symmetrical. Salt crystals have four equal square faces. Gypsum crystals also have four faces but they are **parallelograms**. Quartz crystals are a hexagonal shape.

amethyst geode

TRICKY CRYSTALS

Identifying crystals can be tricky because some minerals take on different shapes depending on how they form. Gypsum forms enormous hexagonal crystals in caves, but in dry deserts it forms desert roses. These are pink crystals shaped like roses that grow when gypsum crystallises around grains of sand in hot conditions. Small crystals of quartz or calcite minerals can grow inwards into spaces within rocks called **geodes**.

desert rose

malachite

Clues to the Past

Malachite minerals grow amazing crystals that are shaped like weird, melted bunches of grapes! This shape is a clue to how the crystals formed long ago. In malachite, layers of minerals containing copper form in bands around a speck of sand, dust or other substance. Over time, many bands of slightly different colour build up. Together, they form a sphere shape. Several spheres grow into each other, creating the 'grapes'.

CRYSTAL COLOUR AND STRENGTH

Malachite is green, rubies are red, amethyst is purple and diamonds are colourless. Using these colour rules, we can spot many different types of crystals. However, not all crystals follow these colour rules!

COLOUR CONFUSION

Emerald is a green form of the mineral beryl. However, only some beryl is green. Other types are red, pink, yellow or blue. Each colour is created by different atoms that are trapped within the beryl crystal. Emerald looks green because of the chromium in its crystals. A blue type of beryl is called aquamarine, and it gets its colour due to the iron trapped inside the crystal. Fluorite also comes in different colours according to which atoms are trapped inside its crystals.

yellow beryl

red beryl

Shine **ultraviolet (UV) light** on some crystals and they glow with weird and wonderful colours! Pink calcite crystals glow red under UV light. As pink calcite crystals grow, tiny quantities of manganese take up space that calcium atoms would normally take up in the calcite. Rhodochrosite is a mineral that looks identical to pink calcite crystals under normal light. However, it does not glow under UV light, proving it is a different type of crystal.

Fluorite crystals glow purple under UV light.

aquamarine beryl

HARD AND HEAVY

Crystals can be confusing because two different types of crystal can look identical, even under UV light. We can tell them apart by testing the hardness of the crystal. Diamond and clear zirconia crystals may look identical, but diamond can easily scratch zirconia because it is harder. Sometimes two crystals look the same and are as hard as each other. Then scientists tell them apart by chipping off a piece of each crystal. The two pieces must be exactly the same size. Scientists then weigh them to compare the crystals' **density**.

FINDING EARTH'S CRYSTALS

The solid rock on Earth contains most of the crystals on the planet. However, they are usually hidden out of sight. Rather than break open many rocks in hope of finding crystals, people need to know where to look.

THE RIGHT PLACES

Geologists search for some crystals in certain types of rocks or settings. Many large crystals of rubies and emeralds are found in magma that slowly cools deep underground, rather than in magma that rises to the surface and quickly cools. Yellow sulphur crystals are often found around the vents (mouths) of volcanoes because they form from gases that come out of the vents.

Clues to the Past

Diamonds are usually buried within a particular rock called kimberlite. The rock formed long ago from magma that carried the rock from deep underground to the surface.

diamond

ROCK BREAK-UP

Natural processes that are part of the **rock cycle** can reveal crystals at Earth's surface. **Weathering** is when acidic rain, ice or heat break even the hardest rocks into tiny pieces. **Erosion** is when wind, rivers and oceans carry the pieces away. This leaves behind the hardest crystals that weather very slowly.

weathered and eroded rock

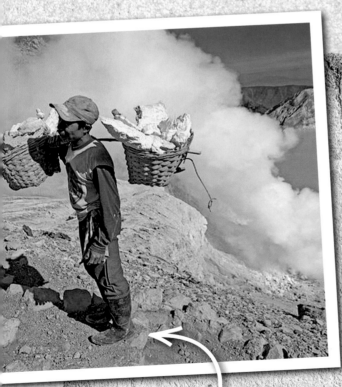

sulphur crystal collector

ROCK STAR STORIES

Blue flames up to 5 metres high shoot from Ijen volcano in Indonesia. The flames appear when sulphur gas deep within Earth catches fire. Ijen has some of the biggest sulphur deposits and largest natural blue flames on Earth. People collect and sell the yellow sulphur, which is made into rubber tyres and sugar.

MINING CRYSTALS

Miners use different techniques to collect crystals. They usually mine where there are large veins of crystals or deposits of many small crystals. It takes time, money and effort to mine. It makes sense to mine where there are many crystals.

CRYSTALS FROM ROCK

Miners use powerful drills and diggers to chip away at the rock around a crystal vein. They dig deep underground to reach more of the crystal, so they build networks of tunnels in which to dig. The tunnels are held up by wooden or metal struts to stop them from collapsing. When miners find hard crystals in rock, like diamond in kimberlite, they crush the rock into smaller

Mechanical diggers are sometimes used to dig up crystal-rich rocks.

and smaller chunks. The diamonds are too hard to be crushed by machines, so only the rock is broken up. Eventually, the rock is crushed into a wet sludge, from which the diamonds can be easily lifted.

CRYSTALS FROM RIVERS

Miners find many crystals, like sapphires, in rivers and streams. The crystals are **deposited** after being eroded from rock elsewhere. Miners scoop up sludge from the riverbed in pans or baskets, then swirl it around to get rid of the mud. When only gravel is left, miners pick out the gems. Some mining companies now use machines to suck up the riverbed sludge and shake away the mud, but people are still needed to spot the valuable crystals.

mine tunnel

ROCK STAR STORIES

The biggest diamond mine in the world is Orapa in Botswana, Africa. It covers about 1 square kilometre. It sits at the top of two kimberlite columns, which were formed when magma from an ancient volcano cooled. Each year, mining machines dig up and crush around 54 million tonnes of rock from Orapa. From this, miners recover around 2.2 tonnes of diamonds!

IMPORTANT CRYSTALS

How many crystals do you use in your everyday life? They may include salt and sugar, but did you also know there are crystals in your computers, televisions and watches? All of these devices and many more rely on crystals.

CRYSTAL SMART

Silicon crystals are an important part of many electronic devices we use every day. Tiny stacks of flat silicon crystals, called **silicon chips**, act like 'brains' in many devices. The layers are printed with very tiny patterns. The patterns are a little like road maps and instructions that direct the movement of power between the layers of the silicon chips. Flat silicon crystals are also sandwiched together to make solar cells. These change the energy in sunlight into electricity.

Solar cells make up solar panels.

In 1927, inventor Warren Marrison created the first quartz clock. When electricity flows through quartz crystal it vibrates exactly the same number of times each minute. Marrison used this property to make the first quartz clock. It was very accurate, but also very large. The first quartz watches were sold in the late 1960s, but they were very expensive. Each clock cost as much as a car!

Diamond crystals cover the tip of this dental drill.

silicon chip

CUTTING THROUGH

Some crystals are used for cutting materials. The steel cutting edges of drills, like those used by dentists to make holes in teeth or miners to dig wells deep into rock, are tipped with tiny diamonds. They give an excellent cutting surface. Lasers are machines that use crystals to direct powerful beams of light that can cut accurately. Doctors use lasers to carry out delicate eye surgery.

PRECIOUS STONES

Crystals that are especially beautiful and hard to find are very valuable. People buy these expensive gemstones for jewellery and as decorative objects.

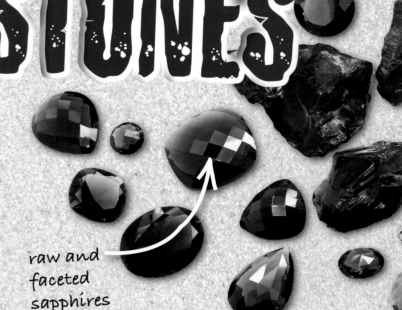

raw and faceted sapphires

PRETTY CRYSTALS

Diamonds, rubies, sapphires and emeralds are among the most expensive gemstones. People set these gemstones in precious metals, such as gold, to make earrings, necklaces and other jewellery. Gemstone workers also cut crystals into shapes to make sparkling animals and figures that people display in their homes.

SHOWING OFF

The most valuable gemstones are those that are very clear and strongly coloured. To make the most of these stones, jewellers

smoky quartz gemstone

use saws to cut a pattern of faces, or flat edges, all over their surfaces. These are called **facets** and they reflect light to make the gemstones sparkle. Jewellers use magnifying glasses while they work to make sure the facets they cut are perfect. After cutting the facets, jewellers also polish crystals to make the flat areas smooth and even shinier.

ROCK STAR STORIES

A plum-sized, perfect pink diamond known as the Pink Star was found in 1999. It is one of the most expensive gemstones in the world. This famous stone was cut and polished for more than two years to reveal its full beauty, and was then mounted onto a ring. In 2013, it sold for £45 million!

Clues to the Past

The ancient Egyptians used crystals for jewellery and to make decorative objects. The crystals found in Egyptian tombs from more than 3,500 years ago tell us about the people buried there. For example, emeralds, rubies, sapphires and diamonds were so rare and highly prized in Egyptian times that people who owned them must have been either royals or very important priests.

emeralds

CRYSTALS ON DEMAND

garnets

Crystals are in high demand in some industries. However, natural crystals of the right size and type may not always be available or may be too expensive to buy. To overcome this problem, people manufacture their own crystals.

GROWING CRYSTALS

Scientists grow some of the large crystals needed to make solar cells, electronics and lasers. A type of garnet is used to make some lasers. To make the crystal, scientists use a powder containing particular **elements**. They melt it at high temperatures to turn the powder into a liquid. Then a machine holds a tiny crystal of the same mineral, called the **seed crystal**, at the surface of the liquid. Layers of crystal start to form around the seed. The machine turns the seed and very, very slowly lifts it up. Over time, a long cylinder of crystal forms around the seed.

Silicon ingots (blocks) are amongst the biggest man-made crystals. These pure silicon giants are cylinders 30 centimetres wide and over 2 metres long. In factories, the ingots are carefully sliced into very thin wafers. These are made into solar cells or silicon chips. In the future, people hope to be able to grow even larger silicon ingots to make more useful devices.

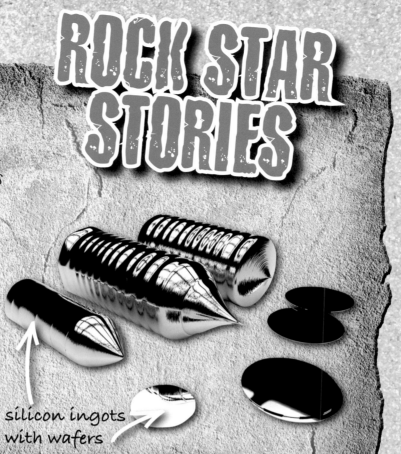

silicon ingots with wafers

UNDER PRESSURE

Scientists make some types of crystals, such as artificial diamonds, by re-creating the very high pressures and temperatures at which they would form naturally deep underground. They put tiny diamond seed crystals inside special presses that weigh hundreds of tonnes. Machines squirt very hot graphite inside the press. Like diamonds, the graphite is made from carbon atoms. The carbon builds up layers around the diamond, making the jewel bigger and bigger.

artificially cut diamond

CRYSTALS IN CRISIS

Crystals are incredible structures that are an essential part of our planet. They are also important resources for use in industry. However, many of the crystals we mine today formed millions of years ago, and very few of some of these crystals are now left. For example, tanzanite is 1,000 times rarer than diamond. It is found only near Mt. Kilimanjaro in Tanzania, Africa.

THE TROUBLE WITH MINING

People need to mine to find certain minerals, but mining is causing damage to the environment worldwide. In some areas, people clear rainforest containing rare animals and plants so they can dig underground in search of crystals. The rock sludge in which miners search for crystals can wash into rivers, and spoil or block them. When miners suck up riverbed gravel in search of sapphires, they destroy fish eggs and many tiny river animals.

The lands around Mt. Kilimanjaro are important for wildlife.

The majority of the world's beaches and deserts are covered with tiny quartz crystals, which form sand. These mini-crystals are the remains of tough rocks, like granite. Most of the minerals that made up the rocks have weathered and eroded away, leaving behind only their light quartz crystals. These are then deposited on land, creating beaches and deserts.

sandy beach

ROCK STAR STORIES

Did you know that crystals are sometimes produced in unethical ways? In some places, crystal miners and gemstone cutters are not paid fairly for their hard work. They also work in dangerous conditions. Sometimes, crystals are mined and sold in order to buy weapons for wars. However, some gem traders are working with the Fair Trade Foundation to make sure that crystal workers have better lives, care for the environment and do not let crystals get into the wrong hands.

gemstone worker

ROCK YOUR WORLD!

Finding crystals is not always easy, so why not grow some amazing crystals of your own?

YOU WILL NEED:

- white wool
- scissors
- two clean, empty jam jars
- small shallow bowl
- two paperclips
- measuring jug
- hot water from the tap
- teaspoon
- baking soda
- food colouring

COMPLETE THESE STEPS:

1. Cut a piece of wool about 1 metre long. Fold it in half and then in half again. Now twist it tightly.

2. Put the two empty jars on either side of the shallow bowl. Then put a paperclip on each end of the length of twisted wool.

3. Put one end of the twisted wool (and its paperclip) into one jam jar and the other end of the twisted wool into the second jar. (The paperclips help hold the wool in the jars.) The wool should curve slightly above the shallow bowl in between the jars. If it does not, adjust the position of the jars until it does.

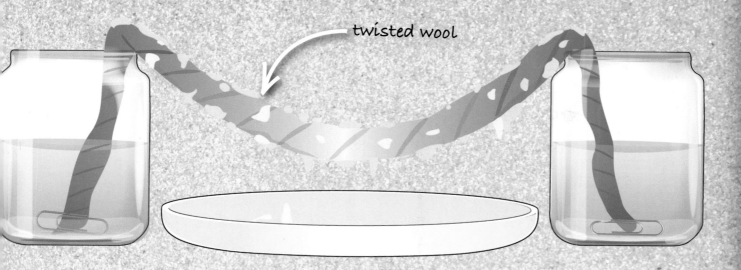

twisted wool

4. Add 500 millilitres of hot water to the jug. Then stir in spoonfuls of the baking soda until no more will dissolve.

5. Add about 15 drops of food colouring to the jug and stir. Then pour enough of this mixture into each jar to cover the ends of the wool.

6. Leave this in a dry, warm place for several days. If a pool of liquid drops into the bowl, empty it back into the jars.

WHAT HAPPENED?

You should be able to see the coloured mixture soaking up into the wool. After about two days, small crystals of baking soda should start to form on the wool. Be patient: after about one week, stalactites should start to grow down from the wool too!

TRY IT OUT!

Take an artifical flower with a paper-wrapped stem and dip it into a jar of borax solution. Ask an adult to help you make the borax solution using borax crystals and hot water. Add some food colouring. See what happens to the petals over the week!

GLOSSARY

acidic When a substance contains chemicals that can readily cause changes in others.

atoms Smallest particles of chemical matter that can exist.

carbon Simple chemical substance.

crystallise Form solid crystals from liquid minerals and other substances.

density Measure of the weight of a standard sized piece of a substance.

deposited Put or set down.

dissolved Completely mixed with a liquid.

elements Simplest chemical substances, like iron or carbon.

erosion When soil and rock are carried away by water or wind.

evaporation The change from a liquid into a gas.

facets Flat sides of a gemstone.

geodes Spaces in rocks lined with crystals.

magma Molten rock usually found beneath Earth's crust.

minerals Solid, naturally occurring substances that make up rocks, soil and many other materials.

molecules Groups of atoms held together.

parallelograms Flat shapes with opposite sides parallel (the same distance apart all the way along) and equal in length.

pressure Pushing force.

rock cycle The constant formation, destruction and recycling of rocks through Earth's crust.

seed crystal A small piece of crystal from which a large crystal of the same material can grow.

silicon chips Tiny pieces of electronic equipment.

solutions Liquids with substances dissolved in them.

symmetrical Having sides or halves that are the same.

ultraviolet (UV) light Rays of light that cannot be seen.

veins Narrow sections of minerals filling gaps in surrounding rocks.

volcanic eruptions When volcanoes send out rocks, ash and lava in explosions.

water vapour Water in the form of gas in the air.

weathering When rock is broken down into small pieces by natural processes.

FURTHER READING

BOOKS

Calver, Paul, and Toby Reynolds, *Rocks, Crystal and Gems* (Visual Explorers), Franklin Watts, 2016

I-Spy. *Minerals, Rocks and Fossils* (I-Spy Books), Michelin Tyre Company, 2012

Riley, Peter, *Rocks and Fossils* (The Curiosity Box), Franklin Watts, 2016/2019

Symes, R.F. *Crystal & Gem* (Eyewitness Guide), DK Children, 2014

WEBSITES

Read about the mineral collection at the Natural History Museum, London, at:
www.nhm.ac.uk/discover/minerals-sparkling-sensitive-and-toxic.html

Watch animations about rock cycle processes, like weathering and erosion, at:
www.learner.org/interactives/rockcycle/change3.html

Watch a short BBC film showing the enormous crystals of the Cave of Crystals at Naica in Mexico at:
www.bbc.co.uk/programmes/p005zh83

INDEX